THIS BOOK BELONGS TO

EVELYN

Welcome to this wonderful
World. We pray that you
grow up to be happy,
healthy and blessed!

Love Great Auntie
Penny ~ Dar.

I dedicate this book to all the parents and caregivers who go to great lengths to help their children fall asleep.

This little lullaby came to me as I was trying to settle one of the many little ones whom I've been lucky enough to have in my care.

Also to my amazing family: Darlene, Cole & Rikki, Bryce and Kaitlynn, and to "Little Sprout"; the announcement of your upcoming arrival inspired me to create this book.

2

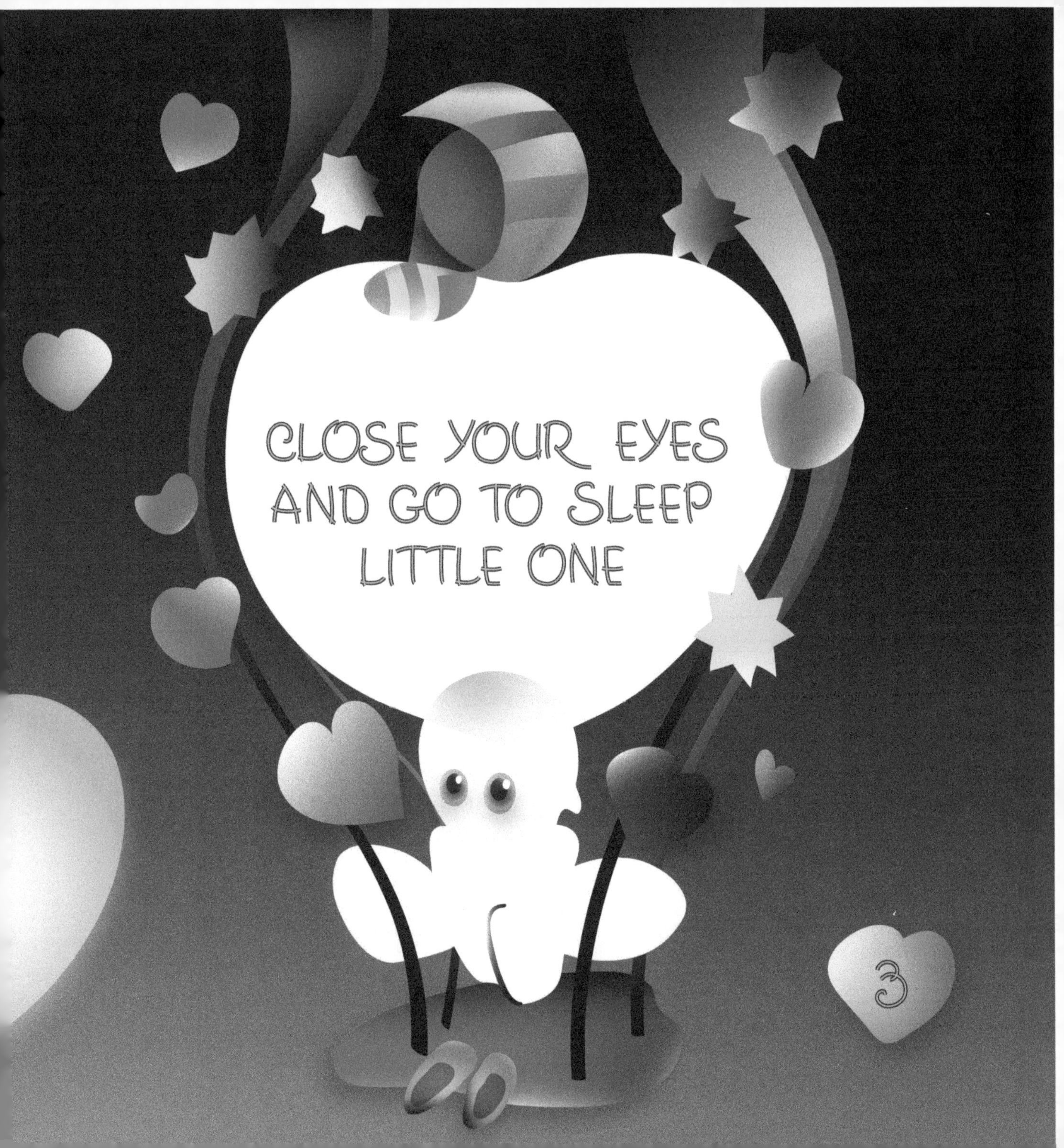
CLOSE YOUR EYES
AND GO TO SLEEP
LITTLE ONE

SILLY MEN
WITH FUNNY HATS

MOMMY LOVES YOU

DADDY LOVES YOU

GRANDMA LOVES YOU

10

GRANDPA LOVES YOU

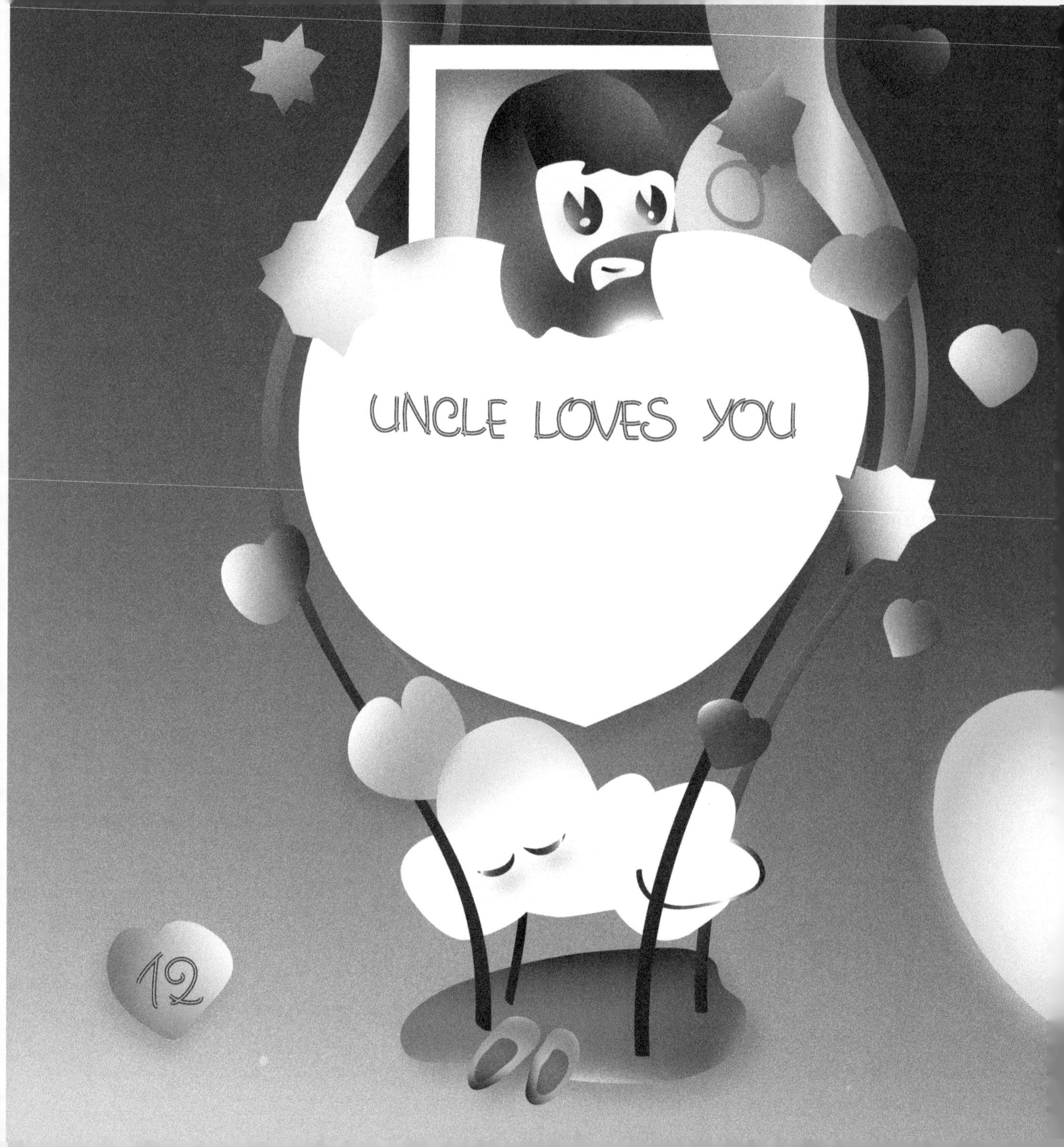
UNCLE LOVES YOU

AUNTIE LOVES YOU

13

GOD LOVES YOU

_____

_____

_____

LOVES YOU

15

CLOSE YOUR EYES
AND GO TO SLEEP
LITTLE ONE

CPSIA information can be obtained
at www.ICGtesting.com
Printed in the USA
BVHW020822121221
620839BV00002B/1